Salvation exposed

Salvation exposed

God's way of salvation

Peter Jeffery

 **EVANGELICAL PRESS**

EVANGELICAL PRESS
Faverdale North Industrial Estate, Darlington, DL3 0PH, England

Evangelical Press USA
P. O. Box 84, Auburn, MA 01501, USA

e-mail: sales@evangelical-press.org

web: http://www.evangelicalpress.org

First published 2001

British Library Cataloguing in Publication Data available

ISBN 0 85234 467 8

Printed and bound in Great Britain by Cox & Wyman Ltd, Reading

Contents

1.

THE WAY IS JESUS

'You are to give him the name Jesus, because he will save his people from their sins'
(Matthew 1:21).

1.

The way is Jesus

The apostle Peter paid a remarkable tribute to the Lord Jesus Christ when he said, 'He received honour and glory from God the Father when the voice came to him from the Majestic Glory, saying, "This is my Son, whom I love; with him I am well pleased"' (2 Peter 1:17). Of course, it was not Peter paying the tribute but God himself. Peter was only reporting what he heard on the Mount of Transfiguration (Luke 9:28-36). If we are concerned to know God's way of salvation then there is no better place to start than here. There can be no greater testimony about God's way than that which comes from God's own lips. God said, 'This is my Son, whom I have chosen; listen to him' (Luke 9:35).

To listen to Jesus must be the best piece of advice ever given to a sinner who wants to know God's way of salvation. There are many voices appealing to our hearts and minds for our attention on the question of the salvation of our soul, so it is not surprising that people get confused. Such confusion will only be dispelled when we follow God the Father's advice and listen to his Son, because Jesus is God's way of salvation.

Who is Jesus?

There is no name from history so frequently upon the lips of people today as Jesus Christ. It is true that often it is used as a curse or swear word, but even then, why the name Jesus? Why don't people use the name Napoleon or Julius Caesar to curse by? Even the blasphemy unconsciously acknowledges Jesus to be different and of greater importance.

In Matthew chapter 16, Jesus is alone with his apostles and he asks them some questions.

'Who do people say the Son of Man is?' (v. 13).

The answer is very interesting. Public opinion held Jesus in high esteem. The people had firm views about him and they were views that were quite remarkable. Some said he was John the Baptist, others that he was Elijah and some believed he was Jeremiah. These three men were dead, but the people believed that God had brought back from the dead one of these great spiritual leaders in the person of Jesus. It was obvious to them that Jesus was no ordinary man and this estimation was based on what they had seen. They had seen the healings and the miracles. They were among those Jesus had fed miraculously with a few loaves of bread and a couple of fish. They had experienced these things and hence their high opinion of Jesus.

High though this opinion was, it was not high enough. In fact, it was wholly inadequate. Jesus was not John the Baptist, or Elijah or Jeremiah. He was and is some-one far greater.

Today's opinions of Jesus are also generally high. Few will dispute that he was a remarkable man. Some say he was a great social reformer, an exceptional moral and religious teacher, a great example of love and humility. But this could be said of many other men. If Jesus was only that, he could not be God's way of salvation for sinners. These views are inadequate and this is why people who hold them do not really take Jesus seriously. They admire his teaching but do not see its relevance in their lives today.

The Christ

Jesus asks another question of his apostles: 'But what about you? Who do you say I am?' (Matthew 16:15).

Peter's answer is that Jesus is 'the Christ, the Son of the living God'. This is a great answer and one that gives sinners hope. 'Christ' is a Greek word, and the Hebrew equivalent was 'Messiah'. But was Peter right to say that Jesus was the long-awaited Messiah, and what led him to say it?

Peter had seen the miracles and healings and this would have contributed to his answer, but it was not the real explanation. Jesus himself gives the reason for Peter's answer in verse 17: 'Blessed are you, Simon son of Jonah, for this was not revealed to you by man, but by my Father in heaven.' Peter had not worked this out for himself but God had revealed it to him by blessing to his heart and understanding the things he had seen and heard. Such a truth is not arrived at by a lucky guess but by divine revelation.

A person can be familiar with the facts about Jesus and still miss the main point that he is the Christ, the Messiah, sent by God to bring deliverance to his people. Facts alone, important though they are, do not save. Saving faith effects not just the mind but the heart as well. Divine revelation is God taking the facts and burning them deep in the heart and conscience so that they become dominant in our understanding and thinking.

What does it mean?

It was the truth of Peter's words upon which Christ built his church. The church was not built on a flimsy, weak and changing character like Peter, but on the truth of who Jesus is.

It means that Jesus is the fulfilment of centuries of promises God had made to sinful men and women. In Genesis 3 man, because of his sin, becomes alienated from God. Left to himself there is no hope for man to change the situation. But there is hope in the promise of God. He promises that sin shall not remain for ever as the conqueror: 'And I will put enmity between you and the woman, and between your offspring and hers; he will crush your head, and you will strike his heel' (Genesis 3:15).

That was the beginning of the gospel and the rest of the Bible is the unfolding and developing of this hope. The promise was vague at first — the offspring of a woman; but the fulfilment was sure — he (Jesus) will crush Satan's head. The promise was as sure as the character of the Promiser. But as time went on, the progress of sin seemed unstoppable. Then at last God sends Jesus the Christ into the world.

Jesus Christ is God's appointed answer to man's greatest problem — the problem of sin.

The prophecies of the coming Messiah in the Old Testament were numerous and varied, but some of the most important are found in Isaiah 53:

Verse 5: 'But he was pierced for our transgressions, he was crushed for our iniquities...'

Verse 6: 'We all, like sheep, have gone astray, each of us has turned to his own way; and the LORD has laid on him the iniquity of us all.'

These prophecies were fulfilled on the cross. Peter himself confirmed this explanation when he said, 'He himself bore our sins in his body on the tree' (1 Peter 2:24).

This means that the guilt and punishment of human sin was borne by Jesus. So who is Jesus?

He is the Saviour; God's one and only provision for our salvation. And as Peter tells us in Matthew 16, he is supremely qualified to be our Saviour because he is 'the Son of the living God'. Not *a* son, but *the* Son. Or as Jesus put it in John 3:16: 'God's one and only Son'.

John the Baptist, Elijah and Jeremiah were men. They were great men but nonetheless men, and, as such, sons of Adam possessing a sinful and depraved nature. Jesus is the Son of God — divine and sinless.

Great men are still sinners and therefore under the wrath and condemnation of God. Jesus stands alone as the God/Man, possessing a divine as well as a human nature. He alone is qualified to be God's way of salvation.

2.

THE ONLY WAY

'And we have seen and testify that the Father has sent his Son to be the Saviour of the world'
(1 John 4:14).

2.

The only way

A young woman in her mid-twenties came into the church one Sunday for the first time. After the service I spoke to her and discovered she was a schoolteacher and a very devout Roman Catholic. 'If you are a Roman Catholic,' I said, 'why have you come here?' She answered, 'I know God but I know nothing about Jesus. I want to learn about Jesus.' I replied, 'You cannot know God without Jesus.' She was amazed at the answer, as many religious people would be, but the Bible is very clear that Jesus is the only way to God.

Given the religious thought of today this truth is unacceptable to many. They regard it as bigoted and a failure to recognize the worth of religions other than Christianity. The prevailing thought is that everyone is entitled to his opinion and that one religious opinion is as good as the next. A more unreasonable and absurd attitude it would be difficult to find. How can several diametrically-opposed teachings on the way to God all be right? It is like a man in Edinburgh asking the way to London and being given the conflicting instructions to take a plane and fly west, take a boat and go east, take a train and go south. If he has any sense he will know that all the answers cannot be right. If he takes the trouble to look at a map he will be able to decide which piece of advice he should follow.

Accepting the truth that Jesus is the only way to God is not intolerant bigotry: it is simply believing the teaching God has given us in his Word. There Jesus said, 'I am the way and the truth and the life. No one comes to the Father except through me' (John 14:6).

Peter said, 'Salvation is found in no one else, for there is no other name under heaven given to men by which we must be saved' (Acts 4:12).

Paul said, 'For there is one God and one mediator between God and men, the man Christ Jesus' (1 Timothy 2:5).

Nothing is more clearly stated in the Bible. The above quotes can bear no interpretation other than that Jesus is the only way to God.

The problem

The way to God and heaven is shut to us by our sin. That sin must be dealt with to God's satisfaction if a way is to be opened for sinners. Sin is a breaking of God's law and a rebellion against the authority of God. It is not merely a moral defect but an affront to the character and holiness of the Lord. Sin is a serious business and God's reaction to it is revealed in Genesis 6:5-6: 'The Lord saw how great man's wickedness on the earth had become, and that every inclination of the thoughts of his heart was only evil all the time. The LORD was grieved that he had made man on the earth, and his heart was filled with pain.'

God cannot be indifferent to sin and his opposition to it is not just that of a judge. His heart is the heart of a loving father pained and grieved by the waywardness of his children. For him to say that he was sorry he ever made man is a staggering acknowledgement. When man sins, God suffers.

Human sin affects the relationship between God and man in two basic ways. Firstly, it brings upon us the wrath and condemnation of God. Secondly, it leaves us totally unable to meet God's requirements of love and obedience to his law and word. If a way is to be opened to God it must deal with both these problems. The way to God must be one that meets with God's full approval and satisfies the demands of God's law. Sin must be dealt with if we are ever to have a happy relationship with God. This problem is immense. It is completely beyond man to solve even though history is full of his perverted ingenuity to obtain divine favour. If there is to be a solution, it is God who must provide it.

God's remedy

In John 3:16 we have a perfect statement of God's remedy for sin: 'For God so loved the world that he gave his one and only Son, that whoever believes in him shall not perish but have eternal life.'

In his divine love God provides a remedy which deals justly with the punishment that sin deserves and yet at the same time provides pardon for the sinner. God has said that the penalty for sin is death — spiritual and physical death. Nothing can change that because it is the judgement of the holy God. God will not turn a blind eye to our sin. Justice must be done, so the demands of God's law and the penalty for breaking that law must be satisfied.

In love and mercy God declares that he will accept a substitute to die in the sinner's place. But God's law demands that the substitute must be free from the guilt of sin and therefore not deserving of death himself. None of us could meet these requirements. So God sent his own Son into the world to become man and to keep his law fully and perfectly. This is what the man Jesus did, and thus became the only acceptable sacrifice to God for human sin.

This is why Jesus is the only way to God.

No other way

In John 14:6, the verse quoted above, Jesus is not saying that he is one of many ways to God but that he is the *only* way. There is a uniqueness and exclusiveness about Jesus when it comes to the matter of our salvation. There is a triple claim in that verse which is quite amazing. Jesus is *the* way and *the* truth and *the* life. There is no alternative to him and the second part of the verse confirms this: 'No one comes to the Father except through me.'

Why is Jesus so adamant that he is the only way to God? The stand he is taking leaves him either totally deluded or totally correct. There is no room for half measure. Either Jesus is deluded and we can safely ignore him, or he is right and therefore it would be the greatest possible folly to ignore him. Our eternal destiny hangs upon this; so do we believe that Jesus is the only way to God?

The facts

How else can sin be dealt with and atoned for, other than through a perfect sacrifice? The sacrificial system set out in the Old Testament points to this, and the book of Hebrews continually draws on the Old Testament to illustrate the meaning of the death of Jesus.

'Now there have been many of those priests, since death prevented them from continuing in office; but because Jesus lives for ever, he has a permanent priesthood. Therefore he is able to save completely those who come to God through him, because he always lives to intercede for them' (7:23-25). Once a priest dies he becomes useless to sinners seeking God's forgiveness. He can offer no sacrifice and make no prayers on their behalf, but Jesus lives for ever, therefore there is no end to his ministry. Time never weakens his ministry. Man is always eventually beaten by time. It is sad to see the skills of a great sports star wane as he goes on too long in the sport and new up and coming youngsters outshine him. That will never happen with Jesus. The salvation he offers sinners today is as effective as that experienced by the thief on the cross.

'The blood of goats and bulls and the ashes of a heifer sprinkled on those who are ceremonially unclean sanctify them so that they are outwardly clean. How much more, then, will the blood of Christ, who through the eternal Spirit offered himself unblemished to God, cleanse our consciences from acts that lead to death, so that we may serve the living God!' (9:13-14). There will always be a limit to what religious observances can do and that limit always stops short of salvation. This is inevitable, but there is no such inevitability about what Christ has accomplished for us. His sacrificial death cleanses the heart, soul and conscience of the repentant sinner.

'Therefore, brothers, since we have confidence to enter the Most Holy Place by the blood of Jesus, by a new and living way opened for us through the curtain, that is, his body, and since we have a great priest over the house of God, let us draw near to God with a sincere heart in full assurance of faith' (10:19-22). Here is a confidence based not on our own efforts but on what God has done for us in the Lord Jesus Christ.

A sacrifice for sin has to be acceptable to God. Nothing but the death of the sinless Jesus Christ, God's only Son, could possibly be acceptable to the holy God. Sin that so grieves the heart of God has to be fully atoned for. 'Christ redeemed us from the curse of the law by becoming a curse for us … He redeemed us in order that the blessing given to Abraham might come to the

Gentiles through Christ Jesus, so that by faith we might receive the promise of the Spirit' (Galatians 3:13-14).

Of no one else does the Bible say, 'For God was pleased to have all his fulness dwell in him, and through him to reconcile to himself all things, whether things on earth or things in heaven, by making peace through his blood, shed on the cross' (Colossians 1:19-20).

In the light of God's clear declarations about Jesus, to look for another way would be like a man with a brain tumour asking a witch doctor rather than a brain surgeon to operate on him.

3.

A SURE WAY

'Everyone who calls on the name of the Lord will be saved' (Romans 10:13).

3.

A sure way

The fact that God has given us one Saviour rather than two or three is a great comfort. If there were alternative ways to God we would always be uncertain as to whether or not we had taken the best way available. That there is only one way, and that way is God's Son, means that all such uncertainty is removed. Jesus is the only way, the best way and therefore a sure way.

In 1992 a cardiologist told me that I had a serious heart condition and that surgery was the only remedy. There was no other way. But who would do the delicate open-heart surgery? I had many good friends but I would not trust them to do it because they did not have the training and skill. I wanted someone with a good track record. Someone who had done the operation before and had patients walking around as proof that he knew his job. The matter was too serious for just anyone to operate on my heart.

The same is true in the matter of salvation. Who can save us? Who is qualified? Who has saved others? The only answer to these questions is Jesus. His track record is perfect. No one has ever come to him in repentance and faith and gone away without salvation. Jesus is the sure way to God.

In his first letter John spells out the certainty of salvation in Jesus and equally affirms that outside of Christ there is no salvation: 'And this is the testimony: God has given us eternal life, and this life is in his Son. He who has the Son has life; he who does not have the Son of God does not have life' (1 John 5:11-12).

God's testimony

In the fifth chapter of his first letter between verses 6 and 12, John uses the word 'testimony' eight times. The word stresses the truth that John wants to bring before us. God has something to say to us because it is his own testimony about his Son.

A testimony is more than opinion or viewpoint. It is a declaration with evidence of what a person knows and has experienced. For instance, when someone gives a testimony of salvation they are relating what they have experienced of God. They are putting forward their own lives as evidence of the transforming power of the gospel. Hearers will not doubt that it is real to the person testifying, but may well dismiss it as 'OK for them but not for me'. They may put it in the same category as a man's excitement experienced at a football match, or his ecstasy on hearing a piece of music by Beethoven. That's alright, they may argue, if you like football or Beethoven, but they do nothing for me.

That can be a reasonable enough argument on a human level but John is not talking of a man's testimony. He is talking about God's testimony, and he argues, 'God's testimony is greater because it is the testimony of God, which he has given about his Son' (v. 9). God has something to say to us about Jesus. This cannot be so easily dismissed as mere enthusiasm. We should listen to what God has to say about Jesus Christ.

God wants us to know who Jesus is

God says that Jesus is his Son. He wants us to see his uniqueness. Jesus is not just another religious leader who may or may not be right. He is the eternal Son of God. This truth alone makes the salvation he brings a certain and sure way to God. Jesus is not a man groping after truth, he *is* the truth. He is God come down to earth to rescue sinners and bring them to himself. The question of who Jesus is, is crucial for our salvation and we will keep coming back to it.

God wants us to know what Jesus did

Why did God become man?

The Bible has only one answer to that. He came to save. It is no accident that God insisted that the name given to his Son when he was born at Bethlehem was Jesus. Jesus means Saviour.

Jesus came to die instead of us. He himself made this truth when he said, 'I [come] to seek and to save what was lost' (Luke 19:10). He also said that he came 'to give his life as a ransom for many' (Matthew 20:28). The Bible says the wages of sin is death (Romans 6:23) — and when Jesus died for guilty sinners he was paid and accepted that wage on our behalf.

The gift

God wants us to know these things because he has a gift for us: 'This is the testimony: God has given us eternal life, and this life is in his Son.' It is often said that in this world you get nothing for nothing. Some super-markets display a sign saying that there is no such thing as a free carrier bag. What they mean is that the cus-tomer will have to pay for it one way or another.

Several years ago the Hoover company offered free flights from Britain to America to anyone who bought one of their appliances. So many folk bought a Hoover product and claimed their free flight that Hoover was unable to meet the demand. An enormous row followed, as customers demanded that Hoover keep its promise. God offers us eternal life and it is really free to us, even though it cost God the death of his Son. And God, un-like Hoover, is able to fully satisfy the demand. We can be sure than none that apply for this free gift will go away disappointed.

What exactly is the gift of eternal life? Jesus tells us in John 17:3: 'Now this is eternal life: that they may know you, the only true God, and Jesus Christ, whom you have sent.' The gift is to know God as Father, Lord and Saviour. It is an introduction to the grace and mercy of the living God.

Many will dismiss this as something not very attrac-tive or appealing. They may say, 'If God were to offer me a vast amount of money then I would be interested.' Such an attitude is all too common and it reveals the desperate need we have. It fails to appreciate what we are. Human beings are not animals with a limited existence upon earth. We are made in the image of God. We are beings with an immortal soul. Life does not end in the grave: there is an eternity before us in either heaven or hell.

The certainty

God's Word says, 'This life is in his Son. He who has the Son has life.' The gift does not merely come through Jesus, it is *in* Jesus. This means that you cannot have the gift apart from Jesus.

Over the summer months people go away on holidays. Most folk just like to sit in the sun, relax, and come back with a suntan. You may see a man with a deep tan that you admire and you ask him where he got it. 'In Spain', he replies. You would like a tan like that so you dash around to the travel agent and get all the available brochures on Spain. Then you go to the library and borrow some travel books on Spain. Lastly you begin to attend night classes to learn Spanish. You do all this and your knowledge of Spain has vastly increased, but you have no suntan. You don't get a tan by learning about Spain; you get it in Spain.

In the same way you can learn lots of things about God and Jesus, but you will only get eternal life *in* Jesus. To be in Christ means to be one with him, to love him and to trust him. It means to rely only upon him for salvation. It means that you are part of him and he is part of you.

Such a gift is too important to be unsure about it. And God never intended that we be uncertain. He says very firmly, 'He who has the Son has life.' That is a certainty. The gift is received by coming to Christ in repentance and faith and asking for it.

Is that too simple? It is what Jesus said: 'Ask and it will be given to you' (Matthew 7:7). If someone told you that he thought you did not look too good and he felt that you needed a holiday, and then he offers you two free weeks in Spain, how would you respond? In all probability you would grab the ticket thankfully.

God says that you need salvation and that it is free in Jesus.

How will you respond?

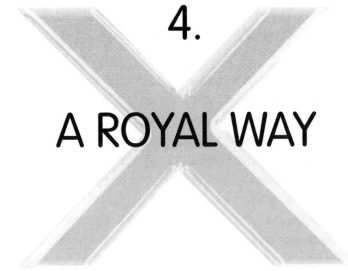

4.

A ROYAL WAY

'"As surely as I live," says the Lord, "every knee will bow before me; every tongue will confess to God"' (Romans 14:11).

4.

A royal way

As God has ordained only one way by which sinners can come to him, it is not surprising that this way is very special. And because the way is not a set of laws but a person, that person must be special. There is nothing ordinary about how a sinner comes to God. Everything about salvation is extra-ordinary and supernatural. The most amazing thing of all is the Saviour himself.

Who Jesus is, is the crux of his qualification to be the only way to God. He is the King of Kings and Lord of Lords. Therefore the way he instigates is a royal way. Everything about the way to God is as staggering and as glorious as Jesus, who is the way.

The next King of England will probably be Charles. People ask what sort of king he will be. Opinions vary but one thing is certain, he will be a constitutional monarch. This means he will be a king who is nice to have around on special occasions, ideal when you need pomp and ceremony, but really a king with no power or authority. A king to fête and applaud now and again, but a king with no real place in the lives of most of his subjects.

Jesus is not a king like that.

It is true that there are many who would like Jesus to be a constitutional monarch — a king nice to have around on a few special occasions like christenings, weddings and funerals, but a king with no authority over us. They would like Jesus to be a king not to be taken too seriously because they don't want Jesus interfering in their daily lives. A constitutional Jesus would please many folk. But he will not have it that way. The King of England must be a constitutional monarch or be no monarch at all. He has no choice in the matter. Jesus is not like that because he has power and authority, and he uses them.

The authority of the king

The kingship of Jesus is portrayed very clearly in the story of the triumphal entry into Jerusalem on Palm Sunday in John 12. The crowd catches something of the wonder of what is happening and they use the words of Psalm 118 to express this: 'Blessed is he who comes in the name of the LORD.'

This is his authority. Jesus is not a king by accident of birth or because an ancestor killed someone or married someone. He is king by the sovereign decree of the Lord God of heaven, and he comes in the name of that Lord.

Jesus is the king who had long been promised. He did not suddenly turn up out of nowhere. God had promised that he would send Christ the King and for centuries the prophets had spoken of him. The description by John of the triumphal entry contained two references from the Old Testament: Psalm 118 verse 13 as quoted above, and in verse 15 a quote from the prophet Zechariah. Isaiah also speaks so graphically about the coming way to God. In chapter 9 he stresses the King's authority: 'For to us a child is born, to us a son is given, and the government will be upon his shoulders. And he will be called Wonderful Counsellor, Mighty God, Everlasting Father, Prince of Peace. Of the increase of his government and peace there will be no end. He will reign on David's throne and over his kingdom, establishing and upholding it with justice and righteousness from that time on and for ever'. Isaiah concludes verse 7 with the words: 'The zeal of the LORD Almighty will accomplish this'; in other words, heaven's glory and authority belong to Jesus.

The ultimate authority, that supersedes all human authority, is that Jesus comes in the name of the Lord. Today that authority is challenged, even ridiculed, and certainly rejected, but one day, 'at the name of Jesus every knee should bow, in heaven and on earth and under the earth, and every tongue confess that Jesus Christ is Lord, to the glory of God the Father' (Philippians 2:10-11).

The power of the king

Historically a king's greatness has been expressed in terms of his power. The all-important questions were: How strong is he? What can he do? What can he accomplish?

John, in the chapter 12 passage, demonstrates the power of Jesus in one devastating phrase, 'Lazarus … whom Jesus raised from the dead'. That is immense power. History is full of kings who killed the living, but Jesus is the only king who raised the dead. History is full of kings who thought their power was greater than it was. King Canute thought he could command the sea but got his feet wet when he ordered the waves to retreat. But there is no limit to the power of King Jesus — even the winds and waves obey him.

Speaking to Lazarus's sisters Jesus describes his power with the remarkable words, 'I am the resurrection and the life. He who believes in me will live, even though he dies.' In the presence of Jesus, death, which conquers all, from kings to slaves, meets its conqueror. He spells the death of death. No wonder Jesus is the only way to God, because who can be compared with him? If he can conquer death then he can be relied upon to be a sure and certain way to God.

The subjects of the king

Jesus tells us that his kingdom is not of this world (John 18:36). Yet even in this world he has subjects who are revealed by their attitude and actions towards him. In John 12 the true subjects of King Jesus proclaim their king as they paved his way and shouted 'Hosanna'.

Perhaps there were some on the first Palm Sunday who were swept along by the excitement and the crowd. If so, Jesus was not deceived because he knows all his subjects by name. Their praise, unashamed adoration and demonstrated love and devotion show them to be true subjects of the king. Those on the true way to God love Jesus with a passion that cannot be hidden.

The enemies of the king

There has never been a human king who did not have enemies. There will always be some who reject his authority and want him off the throne. In John 12 the enemies of King Jesus are evident: 'Meanwhile a large crowd of Jews found out that Jesus was there and came, not only because of him but also to see Lazarus, whom he had raised from the dead. So the chief priests made plans to kill Lazarus as well.'

There are two sorts of enemy revealed here. Firstly, there are the excitement seekers who came only to see Lazarus. They were amazed and excited by what Jesus did but they did not love Jesus. Lazarus was the attraction not Jesus. Such people only remain loyal as long as the miraculous signs keep coming. Their affection can very soon turn to opposition as it did with the people who experienced the eating of the loaves and fishes in John 6 (vv. 26-27). Then there were the religious enemies who hated Jesus and were jealous of the acclamation the people were giving him. Such people never find God because they reject Jesus, the only way to God.

5.

A PLANNED WAY

'In him we were also chosen, having been pre-destined according to the plan of him who works out everything in conformity with the purpose of his will' (Ephesians 1:11).

5.

A planned way

Preaching on the day of Pentecost the apostle Peter explained the cross in terms of both the wickedness of man and the infinite love of God. He accused his hearers very clearly of putting the Son of God to death. Their sin was enormous and they were responsible for it, but overriding this was the plan of God: 'This man was handed over to you *by God's set purpose and foreknowledge*; and you, with the help of wicked men, put him to death by nailing him to the cross' (Acts 2:23).

The death of Jesus, both with regard to its manner and its purpose, was set and determined by God himself. It was not a last-minute adjustment to a plan that was going wrong. It always was the plan, as the many references and allusions to the cross in the Old Testament make very clear. This is a thrilling truth because it puts our salvation at the heart of God's will and purpose for this world. It also reveals the folly of rejecting not merely a doctrine but the set way of almighty God.

The death of Jesus on the cross was planned by God in every detail and over a period of thousands of years he alludes to it in Scripture and shows us it is going to happen. Therefore there should be no doubt as to its meaning, and we had better take it seriously.

Creation

When God created the world he did so meticulously and carefully, so much so that if things were only slightly different life on earth would be impossible. For example, our distance from the sun is exactly right to give earth the correct temperature to sustain human life. If the average temperature of the earth was raised by only two or three degrees, the polar ice sheets would melt and London would be under twenty feet of water. If our planet was 10% smaller or 10% larger, human life could not exist. In the same way the 23.5% tilt of the earth's axis is not some arbitrary thing but necessary for life.

Such meticulous work was needed by God to sustain human life on earth and in the same way when God planned our salvation he was equally painstaking. God's way is the only way and we cannot amend it without fatal consequences. Man is now discovering that his own foolishness and greed is affecting the ozone layer — the barrier God put forty miles above the earth to protect us from the sun's killer rays. We are all aware of the danger to life from a hole in the ozone layer. We cannot play around with God's meticulous plans either in creation or salvation. We need the cross exactly as God planned it. There can be no variation, no amendments and no changes. The cross is God's set purpose and we must accept it as such.

In the garden of Gethsemane the disciples, not understanding what was taking place, tried to prevent the arrest of Jesus by meeting force with force. Jesus stopped them with the warning, 'But how then would the Scriptures be fulfilled that say it must happen in this way?' (Matthew 26:54). Then he makes this statement concerning his coming death, 'But this has all taken place that the writings of the prophets might be fulfilled.' Over and over again the New Testament repeats the same truths and not merely with regard to the general idea of the Saviour's death, but even to specific details such as the betrayal.

Why did God do it?

There are two reasons why God planned our salvation as he did. The first is that he wanted to do it because he loved us. The other reason is that he had to if we were to be saved. Without a Saviour all sinners will perish eternally. Both reasons are found in John 3:16: 'For God so loved the world that he gave his one and only Son, that whoever believes in him shall not perish but have eternal life'.

It is God's love that makes the cross possible and it is God's holiness that makes it necessary. That God is love is a precious truth that is accepted by practically everyone, but the meaning we give to love is not always biblical. Modern man confuses love with sentimentality and sees God's love as a sort of general benevolence that has no other purpose but our happiness. It then follows that God will not punish sin. Consequently every notion of hell is dismissed as incompatible with the idea of a God of love. Such thinking is seriously flawed because though it is true that God is love, this is not the only thing that is true about God. He is also holy. The love of God as seen on the cross saves sinners, but what are they saved from? The Bible has only one answer to that — sinners are saved from perishing, from the consequence of their sin, from the wrath and judgement of God upon that sin. Why, in John 3:16, are people perishing? Because God is holy and will not and cannot tolerate sin.

In 1 John 4:9-10 we see both the love and holiness of God linked together. 'This is how God showed his love among us: he sent his one and only Son into the world that we might live through him. This is love: not that we loved God, but that he loved us and sent his Son as an atoning sacrifice for our sins.' Why was it necessary for Jesus to be an atoning sacrifice or propitiation for our sins? Because God in his holiness had declared that the wages of sin was death. He will not blink at human sin or pretend it is nothing. It has to be dealt with according to his own law. The atoning sacrifice or propitiation Jesus made on the cross satisfies the law of God and thus satisfies his holiness. The word propitiation means that on the cross, bearing our sin and guilt, Jesus faced the wrath of God instead of us, and paid fully on our behalf the debt we owed to the broken law of God. At Calvary God dealt with the problem of sin in the only way that could satisfy his holy justice and enable him to move in and break the power of Satan in sinners' lives.

The fact is that it is the holiness of God that dictates the events on Calvary. In his love God decided to save sinners from the consequence of their sin, but it is God's holiness that dictates exactly how this is done. A way of salvation had to be found that in no way contradicts the character of God. This means that sin must be punished and not just glossed over.

The only way

Sin is essentially a rejection of the character and being of God. It refuses God's way and is an insult to his holiness. It is a hatred of all God stands for. But no person can live in this world apart from the ways of God. God has made us in such a way as to need oxygen to live. If a man puts his head in a plastic bag he will die because there will be no oxygen for him to breath. There is plenty of oxygen all around him but by his action he has chosen to cut himself off from God's provision for life. He deliberately ignores God's way and the consequences are inevitable and terrible.

Similarly God has made a provision for our salvation. If a sinner is to be saved he needs love, grace and mercy, and these flow in abundance from the Lord Jesus Christ. The gospel is not a complicated message only understandable by theologians. It simply says that you are a sinner and Jesus is God's one and only provision for your salvation; believe the gospel; repent of your sin; have faith only in Jesus and live. But many will not do this. They rebel against the meticulously planned way of God and put their heads in a plastic bag called morality or good works or religion.

God's way is the only way but it is a sure way. God planned a perfect and foolproof way of salvation. It can save the young and the old, the clever and the dull, the rich and the poor. No one is barred from it because of race or colour. That way is through the Lord Jesus Christ and is called the gospel.

6.

A UNIQUE WAY

'For it is by grace you have been saved, through faith — and this not from yourselves, it is the gift of God' (Ephesians 2:8).

6.

A unique way

Religious men have always attacked the clear teaching of the Bible on its insistence that there is only one way of salvation. They don't like the exclusiveness of it and challenge the fact that there is only one way to God. In the New Testament Paul faces up to this challenge in his letter to the Galatian church. In the year A. D. 47 he preached in Galatia. This is recorded in Acts chapters 13 and 14. Paul preached Jesus as the only way of salvation and many were saved. A few years later some teachers from Jerusalem came and confused the Galatian believers with the teaching that the grace of God and faith in Christ were not enough for salvation. They said, 'Unless you are circumcised, according to the custom taught by Moses, you cannot be saved' (Acts 15:1).

Paul writes to the Galatians to counteract this. The gospel was at sake: either salvation is by grace or by law. Either Jesus is the only way to God or there is another way.

A different gospel

Paul accuses the Galatians of turning to a gospel that is in fact no gospel at all. This is a strong accusation. If it is no gospel then there can be no salvation in it and sinners are left with no hope and damned to hell. Equally strong is the statement that by rejecting the sufficiency of Christ to save, they are deserting God. Is Paul over-reacting? Is he making a mountain out of a molehill? The answer must be no, because there is no greater issue than the uniqueness and sufficiency of Jesus Christ.

This is always the issue when the matter of the way to God is under discussion. It is the issue between Christianity and the Jehovah's Witnesses, Mormonism and the other cults. It is the issue between biblical Christianity and liberal theology. It is the issue between evangelicalism and Roman Catholicism. It is always the same basic issue because any religion that teaches the necessity of our own efforts or religious rituals as being crucial for salvation does so because it fails to recognize the total sufficiency of the death of the Lord Jesus Christ to save guilty souls.

The key to Paul's argument is in Galatians 1:4: 'The Lord Jesus Christ, who gave himself for our sins to rescue us from the present evil age, according to the will of our God and Father'. It boils down to this — either Christ saves sinners or sinners save themselves. Jesus did not die as a frustrated superstar, or a hero for a cause, or an example of how to endure suffering. The death of Jesus was not even primarily an act of love. It was a sacrifice for sin. Of course love motivated it but essentially, 'Christ gave himself for our sins to rescue us.' It was a rescue operation and it was according to the will of God the Father. In other words, this was God's way of salvation.

That is the gospel. And it is either true or a lie. Any other teaching is a different gospel and is therefore no gospel.

Additions and subtractions

The false teachers causing the trouble in the Galatian church preached a message that sounded like the true gospel. It contained many of the essential truths about Jesus but it added something, and made that something as important as the death and resurrection of Christ. Their addition was the need for circumcision.

All through the centuries false teachers have been doing the same thing. The nature of the addition may change but it always denies the sufficiency of Jesus. The prime result of this is to attack the doctrine of salvation so that the soul is kept from going the way God has ordained. There can be nothing more deadly than that. This is why the strongest language in the New Testament is used against false teachers.

Paul wishes that these men of Galatia could be eternally condemned. Jesus calls such men hypocrites and says, 'They worship me in vain; their teachings are but rules taught by men' (Matthew 15:9). Peter says of the false teachers he confronted, 'These men blaspheme in matters they do not understand. They are like brute beasts, creatures of instinct, born only to be caught and destroyed, and like beasts they too will perish' (2 Peter 2:12). Jude says of these men that they are godless, 'who change the grace of our God into a licence for immorality and deny Jesus Christ our only Sovereign and Lord' (Jude 4).

Today's false teachers vary little from this age-old pattern. The liberal theologians subtract from Scripture by telling us that we can ignore parts of the Bible, and the Roman Catholics and Mormons add to Scripture with their traditions and special books. Either way, the result is a different gospel.

Strength

The strength of the gospel is its uniqueness. There is nothing like it. And of course there can be nothing like it, because it is a message that originates in God. God orchestrates it as he sends Jesus to do what he requires for man's salvation. It is worked out and becomes operative in the life and death of Jesus. God's gospel is Jesus and as such it is unique.

It is not strength but weakness to tolerate other ways to God. The gospel is not debatable. It is to be grasped as the only lifeline for sinners.

The unique plan

In 1976 a plane with 244 passengers was hijacked and flown to Entebbe in Uganda. The Jewish passengers were separated from the others and threatened with death. The authorities in Israel decided to rescue them. An audacious plan was put into action but total secrecy was required. If details leaked out, it would put the hostages in danger and probably foil the rescue plan.

When God decided to rescue his people held captive by sin, he did it differently. He told everyone. The Old Testament was full of the plan and openly declared what the coming Messiah intended to do. God did it this way to encourage his people, and also to demonstrate his confidence in the Rescuer.

When at last Jesus, the Rescuer, came into the world, God sent a choir of angels to announce it and put a special star in the sky to proclaim it. The rescue was not by a planeload of heavily armed soldiers, but by a baby. The devil must have thought that his work was being made easy. All he had to do was to kill the baby and the rescue plan was thwarted. But even baby Jesus was too much for Satan.

After the Rescuer's birth, nothing happened for thirty years; then Jesus began to preach and heal the sick. From then on, the sole intention of hell was to stop Jesus. The temptation in the wilderness was part of this, but Satan's main card was played when he entered into Judas Iscariot's heart and made him betray Jesus. The religious leaders became part of the plan to foil God's rescue bid when Jesus was crucified.

Satan was pleased and must have thought that this was the end of God's plan. Foolish Satan! The death of Jesus was God's rescue plan, and the resurrection proved it. Jesus rescued his people. He paid the debt they owed and purchased their salvation.

What a plan! It was unique. Nothing can compare with it. To look for another way is to be spiritually blind.

7.

A NARROW WAY

'Make every effort to enter through the narrow door, because many, I tell you, will try to enter and will not be able to' (Luke 13:24).

7.

A narrow way

In the Sermon on the Mount, Jesus tells us that the way to God is a narrow way: ' Enter through the narrow gate. For wide is the gate and broad is the road that leads to destruction, and many enter through it. But small is the gate and narrow the road that leads to life, and only a few find it' (Matthew 7:13-14).

The sermon really finishes at verse 12 of chapter 7 and from then on Jesus applies it to his listeners. It is as if he is saying, 'You have heard the sermon, now what are you going to do about it?' Having heard the Word of God, a reaction is demanded by Jesus. God's Word is not meant to entertain or merely to give us a warm glow inside, it always demands a response. You either accept it or reject it. There is no halfway response and this is illustrated in what Jesus said about the broad and narrow way. No one can have one foot on each way at the same time. It has to be one or the other for us all.

Jesus pictures two gates, one is wide and the other narrow, and these lead onto two ways which again are wide and narrow. Jesus does not say that we must choose one of the two gates and enter through it. He only says, 'Enter through the narrow gate.' This is because all men and women are already on the wide road. We have gone through the wide gate and by nature we are on the way that leads to destruction.

There are only two ways through life and we must be on one or the other. The situation is not that we are going through life innocent and happy, and suddenly we are confronted with a fork in the road and must decide which way to take, the narrow way or the wide way. Rather we are all on the wide road, going with the crowd along the way of the world. Then by the grace of God the gospel is brought before us, and this presents us with an opportunity to get off the way that leads to destruction.

In the Word of God we are confronted with Jesus. There is no neutrality offered us, we are called to come to him, to enter through the narrow gate and begin a new life on a new way with a new destination. The choice is to stay on the way we have always been on, or to go God's way.

The broad way

This road is wide, attractive and very popular. There are none of the rules and laws you find for instance in the Sermon on the Mount. You can be religious or irreligious, moral or immoral. It does not matter because nothing is right and nothing is wrong. There are no standards and no absolutes. If you want to do something, then do it, because no one can tell you that you are wrong.

No wonder this way is popular; but the problem with the broad way is that it is a deception that leads to destruction. It is a lie because there are absolute standards. All men and women must answer to God and he has given us his absolute standards in the Bible. These are not to be debated as if they are human opinion that can be amended or rejected. These are the laws of God for all men and women. Our problem is that we fail to keep them. It is convenient then for those on the broad way to pretend that God's laws are irrelevant; but even the broad way will come to an end, and at the end is God — not God as Saviour but God as judge, and he will pay out the wages of sin, which is death.

The narrow gate

The narrow way is not a way for nice respectable people as distinct from criminals and drunkards. It is a way for sinners, but sinners who know what they are. Sinners who grieve that they fail to keep God's law. Sinners to whom their own personal sin is the greatest sin in the world. Sinners who are sick of their sin and look to Jesus alone to save them.

When they hear the Word of God they respond to it with repentance and faith, or as Jesus put it, they enter through the narrow gate. Jesus uses this description because there are not half a dozen alternative ways to begin on the narrow way. There is only one point at which we can enter and it is the same for everyone. It is the same for a cultured, educated, religious man brought up in England as for an ignorant native in some South American jungle. We enter through Jesus Christ.

The narrow gate is like a turnstile which people have to enter one at a time. It is not the sort of entrance crowds can flock through, but, as we shall see in the next chapter, it is a personal way. And because it is narrow we have to leave behind a lot of baggage that we accumulated on the broad way. Worldliness, pride and selfishness are the sort of luggage not allowed through this gate. In other words, Jesus is warning against an easy salvation that allows a sinner to make a decision for Christ and then go on living as he always did. Salvation means a break with the world. There is no bypassing conviction of sin and repentance when a sinner is saved.

The narrow way

God's way is narrow and therefore difficult. It is not easy being a Christian. Apart from the fact that you are always in the minority, you get misunderstood and opposed. Just consider the standards of the Christian life taught by Christ in the Sermon on the Mount. By the world's standards this is narrow in the extreme, but God means it to be narrow. We just cannot do our own thing. We are to live as Christ himself lived. That is the standard and it is not easy.

It is narrow, but also wonderful, for it gives a sense of direction and purpose that cannot be known outside of Christ. It is a way of peace and satisfaction. In Philippians, Paul evaluates both ways and from his own experience of them says, 'But whatever was to my profit I now consider loss for the sake of Christ. What is more, I consider everything a loss compared to the surpassing greatness of knowing Christ Jesus my Lord, for whose sake I have lost all things. I consider them rubbish, that I may gain Christ' (3:7-8).

The narrow way leads to life, to God and to heaven. The reality of the power of sin is not described anywhere in Scripture more graphically than it is by Jesus when he says that only a few find the narrow way. Few find because few seek. Most people are content to live without God. They are blinded by the bright lights of the broad way and see no need of God. Spiritual blindness is a terrible disease.

By the grace of God the narrow way is still open. Compared to the broad way it is not popular and few walk it, but it is the way that leads to God.

8.

A PERSONAL WAY

'No one can come to me unless the Father who sent me draws him' (John 6:44).

8.

A personal way

We have seen that the entrance to God's way of salvation is through the narrow gate. Among other things, this means that those who enter must enter one at a time. Salvation is not a group activity but something deeply personal as God deals with each of us in mercy and love. There were 3000 saved when Peter preached at Pentecost, and that was not mass hysteria because, as in every act of salvation, those 3000 were saved one at a time. It is because of this truth that it is impossible to inherit salvation. A man's parents may be walking on God's way and he himself on the broad way. God has no grandchildren. Every man and woman has to seek the Lord for themselves and know personally the joy of forgiveness of sin.

He loved me

If you were to ask the apostle Paul how he became a Christian, he would give the glory to Christ and speak of 'the Son of God, who loved me and gave himself for me' (Galatians 2:20). He would tell you not what he did in order to make himself a Christian, but what Christ did for him.

There are many occasions when Paul delights in the breadth of God's love, but at other times he is pleased to remind himself that God's love also focuses upon us as individuals — he loved me. This is the heart of the gospel and the most amazing of all truths. The gospel is a personal message and it comes to each of us as individuals. It is God dealing with me and my own sin. It takes it out of the general and makes it particular. It is when we see it as particular that the message becomes real to us.

Each one of us is different yet the gospel is measured to exactly meet our needs. We might think our whole background would make it impossible for us to be saved. When Paul said, 'He loved me', he could never forget how at one time he was so bitterly opposed to the gospel and tried to destroy the work of Christ. Yet in spite of that, God loved him. The gospel is for sinners and there is no one beyond the reach of the grace of God.

Perhaps you think you do not need saving because your life is not too bad. It may be your boast that you are as good as the next man. Many people are like this and if God were to leave us with these spiritual blinkers on, we would be on the wrong way for ever.

By name

In John 10 when Jesus uses the illustration of the shepherd and his sheep to show the relationship between God and his people, he says, 'He calls his own sheep by name.' This is the striking example of how personal salvation is.

A man hears the gospel and he may be slightly interested, or indifferent, or bored, but it does nothing for him. It leaves him as it finds him — a sinner under the judgement of God. As the years go by he hears the gospel many times and becomes what the Bible calls 'hardened' to it. It becomes very familiar and he knows the truth but is still not saved. Then, for no reason that he can understand, the message begins to bite into his conscience. He finds himself listening, as he has never listened before. He is disturbed and uncomfortable. He thinks the preacher is getting at him and publicly exposing his sins. He doesn't like what is happening to him and vows to stop attending church. But he keeps going back and is convicted of his sin. There grows in his heart a deep longing for Jesus to be his Saviour.

Nothing else seems to matter. What is happening to this man?

God is speaking to him personally and calling him by his name. It can happen the first time a person hears the gospel or after many years of being exposed to God's truth.

The voice of God comes through the gospel. God speaks to the sinner's conscience and creates a sense of guilt. When that happens, being as good as the next man becomes totally irrelevant. The sense of personal sin, personal guilt and personal rebellion against God becomes dominant. The intensity of this conviction will vary from one individual to another, but it will be there to some degree in every sinner God is dealing with. It is this conviction that leads to repentance, and there can be no salvation without conviction and repentance. These silence our protests as to our innocence, and in the language of Romans 3:19, every mouth is silenced. It is then that we see our need of salvation and God shows us that Jesus is the only Saviour. The truth that Jesus 'loved me and gave himself for me' is an enormous relief to a sinner under conviction.

Personal

In John 11 we are told the story of Lazarus. He died and had been in the grave four days when Jesus came to the cemetery in Bethany. The Saviour 'called in a loud voice, "Lazarus, come out!"', and Lazarus was raised from the dead.

Many years ago a preacher said of this incident, 'Jesus called Lazarus by name; if he had not, every corpse in the cemetery would have come out of their graves.' The point he was making was that Jesus had the power to raise every dead body in Bethany, but at that moment he was dealing only with Lazarus.

It is the same with salvation. We are all dead in sin but God raises us one at a time. He calls us by name thus making our salvation very personal and very precious.

9.

A WAY OF GRACE

'[Those who believe] are justified freely by his grace through the redemption that came by Christ Jesus' (Romans 3:24).

9.

A way of grace

The fact that Jesus loved me could not in and of itself save me. Thank God that Paul is able to go on and say, 'and gave himself for me'. Here is love leading to grace and mercy; love issuing in a great act of sacrifice.

In Ephesians 2:4-5, three great gospel words are used: 'But because of his great love for us, God, who is rich in mercy, made us alive with Christ even when we were dead in transgressions — it is by grace you have been saved.' Love, mercy and grace all speak of something God does. Out of God's love flow mercy and grace. Mercy is God not giving us what we deserve, and grace is God giving us what we do *not* deserve. Because of our sin we deserve punishment, but instead God gives us pardon. The last thing we deserve is salvation but in grace God saves us.

Grace is not some vague notion but is a definite act on the part of God. It is God doing for the sinner what no one else could do and what the sinner could never earn or merit. Grace is a unique work of God and it is a completed work. It could never be improved upon. The grace of God in the gospel is as perfect as anything can be. Even God himself could not improve upon the grace he has shown us in Jesus Christ.

It is the love of God that makes Calvary possible, but it is the holiness of God that makes it necessary. Grace flows out of divine love and fully satisfies God's holiness. When grace begins its work it never forgets the absolute holiness of God, therefore it has to provide for the sinner a salvation that does not gloss over or minimize the effect of sin. There must be no short-cut salvation; no salvation on the cheap; no theoretical dealing with sin. God's holiness cannot be deceived or satisfied with such things. The objective of grace is not merely to make sinners accept God, but to make it possible for the holy God to accept sinners.

How does it do this?

The riches of God's grace provide a sacrifice for sin of immense value. It is the quality of the sacrifice that satisfies God's holiness: 'In him we have redemption through his blood, the forgiveness of sins, in accordance with the riches of God's grace' (Ephesians 1:7);

'But now in Christ Jesus you who once were far away have been brought near through the blood of Christ' (Ephesians 2:13).

The sacrifice is Christ, and the key word in both the above verses is 'blood'. The riches of grace are seen in the infinite value of the sacrifice it provides. God gave his best for sinners. God gave his Son to atone for our rebellion. God did this because only the blood of Christ could fully pay the debt that human sin had incurred.

God's holiness demanded that sin should be dealt with justly and legally. That meant that it should be punished and the punishment required was death, separation from God. There could be no salvation without this requirement being fully met. God's grace provides the answer in making Jesus responsible for our sin. God lays that sin upon Jesus and with the sin goes the guilt, and with the guilt goes the punishment.

The word 'blood' means the sacrificial, atoning death of Jesus on the cross when he died as our substitute. It is grace alone that gives the sinner hope and because salvation is by the free grace of God in Christ, there is hope for us all. Grace is for sinners and we are all sinners. This is the hope of the gospel and God's way of salvation.

How do we benefit from grace?

The answer to this crucial question is also found in Ephesians 2: 'For it is by grace you have been saved, through faith — and this not from yourselves, it is the gift of God — not by works, so that no one can boast' (vv. 8-9).

Grace comes to us through faith. We are not saved *by* faith but *through* faith. It is the channel by which the saving grace of God comes to sinners. Faith is not some false optimism or misplaced self-confidence. Neither is it something vague or indefinite. It looks towards what God has done for us in the Lord Jesus Christ. It is not a step into the dark but a step out of the dark into the light. It responds to the light of gospel truth that God brings to our hearts and minds.

Faith throws itself upon the mercy and grace of God. The only reason for the existence of faith is grace. What God has done is the only thing worth putting your faith in. Faith trusts that what Jesus did in dying for sinners is enough to satisfy the holiness of God and the demands of divine law. Faith is believing God and calling upon Jesus for forgiveness and salvation.

True faith

There are many imitations of faith but true faith always has two essential qualities.

It trusts *only* in Jesus. It is not Jesus plus my own efforts or plus anything else. Faith gets to the heart of the issue, which is: What does the sinner need to be acceptable to God? Jesus as our Saviour is all we need, *therefore faith rests in Jesus alone.*

Secondly, faith motivates a response to God's gracious invitation in the gospel. It brings us to Christ in repentance and enables us to receive the free gift of salvation. We read in Acts 11:21 that 'a great number of people believed and turned to the Lord'. The evidence that their faith was real was that they acted upon what they believed and turned to the Lord for the grace of salvation.

Several years ago I received an invitation to go and preach in the USA. I accepted the invitation and after a while an airline ticket was sent to me. The invitation had come from some Christians in America and then they provided the means for me to get there. I could not accept until I was invited, and the invitation would have been hollow unless the means were provided for me to get there. That ticket sat on my desk for weeks. It was all paid for. Everything had been done to make it possible for me to get to America. The only thing that remained was for me to exercise some faith. I had to believe the ticket was genuine and that it was all that was needed to make the invitation a reality. And lastly I had to take the ticket, go to the airport and board the plane.

God has graciously invited you to come to him for salvation. He has given strength to his invitation by sending Jesus to pay the price of your sins. The grace of God has provided all the means for you to be saved. The new birth and faith are gifts that God gives us and he expects us then to believe and come to him in repentance. Faith is an activity of the sinner, not God. In faith we trust in all that God has done for us in the Lord Jesus Christ.

10.

AN OPENED WAY

'For through him we both have access to the Father by one Spirit' (Ephesians 2:18).

10.

An opened way

When Jesus was crucified several remarkable physical phenomena took place. If any single one of these happened today it would make the front page of most newspapers. But at Calvary all three happened almost at the same time. There was a total darkness from 12 noon until 3.00pm; an earthquake; and many dead people were raised to life. All these are recorded in Matthew 27:45-53. The people who were in Jerusalem and experienced these things must have wondered what was happening. Few probably realized that this was the activity of God. But we are told that at least one man realized these events were connected to the death of Jesus. The Roman centurion in charge of the crucifixion said, 'Surely he was the Son of God.'

There was a fourth event that was nothing like as dramatic as the other three but was of far more spiritual significance to those who want to know the way to God: 'At that moment the curtain of the temple was torn in two from top to bottom' (Matthew 27:51). In the middle of recording the events of the death of Jesus, Matthew, Mark and Luke suddenly break off their report to mention a curtain being torn about half a mile from Calvary. It seemed so insignificant and out of place but clearly it was of great significance to the three Gospel writers. Matthew says, 'At that moment', meaning at the exact moment Jesus died, this curtain was torn.

Matthew, Mark and Luke saw this as the clearest sign as to the meaning of the events taking place on the cross. To them it signified that the way to God was being opened up and the God-imposed barriers were now being pulled down by God himself.

The tabernacle

The veil was originally part of the Old Testament tabernacle, which was a sort of portable church that the Jews carried with them during their wilderness wanderings. The tabernacle had been designed by God himself and he gave very detailed instructions to Moses as to how it was to be built (Exodus 25-31).

In the tabernacle there were two rooms, the Holy Place and the Most Holy Place. The Most Holy Place contained only one thing: the Ark of the Covenant with its lid of solid gold, which was called the mercy seat. The curtain separated these rooms (Exodus 26:31-37). The curtain or veil was woven in strands of purple, blue and scarlet onto a white linen background and measured 15 feet by 13.5 feet (4.5 metres by 4 metres). The significance of the curtain was that no one was allowed past it into the Most Holy Place except the High Priest, and even he was only allowed to pass once a year on the Day of Atonement, carrying the blood of the sacrificial lamb that was to be sprinkled on the mercy seat to appease the wrath of God. The curtain barred the way to the Most Holy Place where God was deemed to dwell.

When the wilderness wandering ended and the Israelites settled in the Promised Land, eventually King Solomon built a great temple patterned on the tabernacle. This included the Holy Place and the Most Holy Place separated by the curtain, and exactly the same laws concerning the High Priest and the Day of Atonement. By the time of Jesus, Solomon's temple was gone but Herod's temple replaced it, again with the curtain keeping people out of the Most Holy Place.

In effect the curtain said, 'Keep out'. It barred everyone, except the High Priest once a year, from the mercy seat and the presence of God. Worship and sacrifice took place all around the temple but the curtain barred the people from the essential presence of God. Then at the exact moment when Jesus died, the curtain was torn from top to bottom. It did not wear out, nor was it an accident or an act of vandalism by men. God tore it — from top to bottom.

It meant accomplishment

On the cross Jesus said, 'It is finished.' He was not referring to his life being ended but to God's plan of salvation being completed. We have seen that God's way of saving sinners was no last-minute thought, but a meticulously planned way that the Old Testament Scriptures pointed to. Now this plan was finished or accomplished. The tearing of the curtain proclaimed the end of the old covenant and the beginning of the new.

It was a sign that the Old Testament sacrificial system was no longer needed. Its work of pointing to the Christ was done. There was no longer any need of priest, sacrifices and altars. Jesus the true High Priest had appeared. Jesus the Lamb of God was the last sacrifice that God accepted, and the cross was the last altar needed. To maintain a priesthood and altar now is to deny the accomplishment of Calvary.

Hebrews 7:24-25 tells us that 'because Jesus lives for ever, he has a permanent priesthood. Therefore he is able to save completely those who come to God through him.' Two reasons are then given for Christ's unique ministry as our priest and sacrifice:

1. 'Because he always lives to intercede for them' (v. 25).
2. 'He sacrificed for their sins once for all when he offered himself' (v. 27).

At Calvary something glorious and wondrous has been accomplished and the torn curtain proclaims it. Everything now is different:

No blood, no altar now:
The sacrifice is o'er;
No flame, no smoke ascends on high,
The lamb is slain no more.
But richer blood has flowed from nobler veins,
To purge the soul from guilt and cleanse the reddest
stains.

We thank thee for the blood,
The blood of Christ, thy Son;
The blood by which our peace is made,

The victory is won;
Great victory o'er hell and sin and woe,
That needs no second fight and leaves no second
     foe

(Horatius Bonar).

It meant access

The curtain separated men from God. It pronounced
that no one was worthy to come into his presence. The
only exception was the High Priest as the people's rep-
resentative. This concession of divine grace only served
to further underline that sinners were not welcome. The
people all knew this. They knew that the Most Holy Place
was barred to them and so the reality of God's presence was far removed. But now, 'Therefore, brothers,
since we have confidence to enter the Most Holy Place
by the blood of Jesus, by a new and living way opened
for us through the curtain, that is, his body, and since
we have a great priest over the house of God, let us
draw near to God with a sincere heart in full assurance
of faith' (Hebrews 10:19-22).

We can now draw near to God because God himself
has removed the barrier. The Most Holy Place and the
mercy seat are opened to all sinners who trust in Jesus

as God's only way of salvation. There is now no 'keep out' curtain, but rather the gospel invitation to draw near. Access to God has been bought for us by the death of Jesus.

The curtain symbolized what really keeps us from God, which is our sin: 'Your iniquities have separated you from your God; your sins have hidden his face from you, so that he will not hear' (Isaiah 59:2). But on the cross Jesus dealt with our sin and as a result, 'now in Christ Jesus you who once were far away have been brought near through the blood of Christ' (Ephesians 2:13).

This is God's way of salvation.

It meant acceptance

The curtain said, 'Keep out, you have no place here because you are not acceptable to God.' The tearing of that curtain proclaims a different message: 'When Christ came as high priest of the good things that are already here, he went through the greater and more perfect tabernacle that is not man-made, that is to say, not a part of this creation. He did not enter by means of the blood of goats and calves; but he entered the Most Holy Place once for all by his own blood, having obtained eternal redemption' (Hebrews 9:11-12).

Jesus has obtained for us eternal redemption. In other words, he has made the guilty sinner acceptable to God by covering our sin and paying our debt. In the Lord Jesus Christ, and in him alone, we are acceptable to God. The Lord has opened up a way for us to come to him.

God's immediate confirmation that he accepts Christ's death in the place of guilty sinners is the tearing of the curtain. The great and glorious confirmation of the resurrection had to wait for another three days, but immediately Jesus died, the curtain was torn. We might possibly say that it is as if God, with loving and eager delight, cannot wait three days, so he tears the veil immediately.

The way to God is open and God's invitation to sinners is to draw near.

11.

A REASONABLE WAY

'Review the past for me, let us argue the matter together; state the case for your innocence'
(Isaiah 43:26).

11.

A reasonable way

God's way of salvation is unique and supernatural. It is contrary to all the religious thinking of men but it is not unreasonable. If we always keep in mind the two crucial elements of the God and man relationship, namely, the holiness of God and the sinfulness of man, then God's way is reasonable and the only way that will work. We can see this clearly by looking at the first chapter of Isaiah and heeding God's invitation to reason with him (v.18).

The name Isaiah means 'the Lord is salvation', and that is the theme running right through the book. The first chapter is an introduction to what follows and contains the main themes of Isaiah's message, which he repeats time and time again.

verses 2-8:   The sinfulness of the people
verses 16-19:   Tender approaches from God to the
                people

The invitation to reason with God comes among a se-
ries of tender appeals God makes to the people. He
has accused them of great sin, 'Ah, sinful nation, a
people loaded with guilt, a brood of evildoers, children
given to corruption! They have forsaken the Lord; they
have spurned the Holy One of Israel and turned their
backs on him.' Then in verses 10-11 God says he is
weary of their empty ritualistic worship. In verse 15 we
read of a devastating consequence — God will no longer
listen to their prayers. We can see how seriously God
takes sin. He is really angry with these people but even
with the anger there is mercy. A desire for sin to be
dealt with and the people restored to God is seen in
verse 18: '"Come now, let us reason together," says
the Lord. "Though your sins are like scarlet, they shall
be as white as snow; though they are red as crimson,
they shall be like wool."'

Invitation

God is angry but the invitation is couched in gentle and
gracious words, 'Come now'. This 'brood of evildoers'

who have 'forsaken the Lord' are graciously invited to come and reason with him. Here is something amazing. The Lord of creation is prepared to reason with his creatures. But we must bear in mind all that God has said before the invitation. God is inviting sinners to reason with him concerning his accusations. He is not willing to entertain the possibility that he may be wrong or unjust. He is God and that could not be. God's purpose is that they may see the truth and see also that though he is angry, this loving God wants to show mercy. He wants the matter settled.

It is interesting that in the invitation the people's sins are not described as black but rather as scarlet and crimson. Their sins are blood red, a deep stain that almost defies cleansing. But there is cleansing so that even these sins can be as naturally white as snow or wool.

Isaiah was writing 2700 years ago but the message is still relevant today. Man is still a sinner. God is still the same holy God and he is still the only source of salvation.

Reason

The invitation is to reason with God. The Christian is not afraid of reason. In fact, the Bible is always calling upon people to think and consider. The problem is that generally the sinner will not do this. He will not reason together with God, but is happy to make pronouncements about God — Why does God allow war? Why doesn't God do something about the suffering in the world? These sorts of questions are all too common but men will not take seriously what God says.

Men and women are full of preconceived notions and half-thought-out views about God. They may never read the Bible but are quick to make judgements about it. It seems that everyone is an expert on God and feels entitled to make pronouncements in which reason and knowledge are ignored. A scientist, well known on TV, told children on a radio programme why he was an atheist. It was because as a scientist he had to prove something before he could accept it. He could not prove the existence of God so he could not believe in God. A few years later on a TV chat show he was asked if he believed there was life on other planets. His answer was that though he could not prove it, he did believe there was life out there. So much for scientific reason and objectivity.

In his invitation God is not inviting us to reason about his existence, about the truth of Scripture or about science and the Bible. It is possible to do all these things, but God is concerned here with something more personal and serious. He wants us to reason with him about his view of man and his accusations against us.

God's accusation

The accusation is stated in verses 2-4: 'Hear, O heavens! Listen, O earth! For the LORD has spoken: "I reared children and brought them up, but they have rebelled against me. The ox knows his master, the donkey his owner's manger, but Israel does not know, my people do not understand." Ah, sinful nation, a people loaded with guilt, a brood of evildoers, children given to corruption! They have forsaken the LORD; they have spurned the Holy One of Israel and turned their backs on him.'

Most people would respond to the accusation by acknowledging that no one is perfect and that we all make mistakes, but surely God is going too far in tarring us all with the same brush. Child molesters and drug pushers must be more sinful than those who are guilty of envy, pride and gossip.

This is a good place to start our reasoning but we must first define clearly what we mean by sin. Is sin the variable, changing attitude of what is currently acceptable to society, or is it defined by the unchanging standards of God? If it is the first, then we will see nothing wrong with hundreds of thousands of babies being killed and calling it abortion. In the same way, it would be all right for contraceptive pills to be given to young teenage girls without their parents' knowledge. Homosexuality and adultery are also permissible, for by the first definition they are not sin.

The trouble is that most of us, though we like to think of ourselves as modern and broad-minded, are not really happy with the first definition. We profess to accept it and it is all right as a definition of right and wrong until our teenage daughter gets pregnant or our spouse commits adultery. We apply a double standard. It is all right in theory but terrible if it touches us personally. This is because we are creatures made in the image of God and we know that sin is really a violation of the unchanging standards of God. And by that standard we are all guilty.

Sin is as defined by the Bible, not by politicians or the whims of society. And the greatest sin the Bible knows is the sin of unbelief. It is this that leads to the rebellion and forsaking of God that Isaiah 1:2-4 is referring to. This rebellion is equally true of a man considered moral by society and of a criminal. To fail an exam by one mark or fifty is still to fail.

God's standards are not basically moral or social but spiritual. The spiritual will contain the moral and social, but unless a man knows and loves God, nothing else will be right. This is why a man can be concerned about the environment, be kind to animals, be very concerned about the underprivileged and still fail at the basic relationship of being a good husband.

When we talk about good people, we judge all the time by outward standards; but God looks at the heart. The heart and mind, the secret thoughts and hidden lusts are all open to God and by this standard God's accusation is reasonable and true.

Getting right with God

Let us now reason about man's attempt to get right with God. For most people this attempt boils down to formal religious activities. But God says that formal, nominal religion is useless. In Isaiah 1:11-15 he is quite devastating in his rejection of this — I have had enough of it; I take no pleasure in it; I cannot bear it; I am weary of it and my soul hates it.

This sort of language coming from God himself will shock the person whose whole religious experience surrounds the formal outward worship denounced here. But it is not difficult to see why God feels like this. This whole procedure is empty and has no bearing on life.

Here is a very simple test of your worship. Does what you do in a religious building affect your daily living? Does it affect your family life? When you have crucial decisions to take, is your prime concern what God's will is in the matter?

If we bring a bit of reason to our rituals, we will perhaps begin to see them as God sees them.

God's answer

God's answer is in verse 18-20 and is both reasonable and unanswerable: '"Come now, let us reason together," says the LORD. "Though your sins are like scarlet, they shall be as white as snow; though they are red as crimson, they shall be like wool. If you are willing and obedient, you will eat the best from the land; but if you resist and rebel, you will be devoured by the sword." For the mouth of the LORD has spoken.'

Here is the offer of a fresh start with complete pardon for past failure, and reason should tell us that this is an offer too good to refuse. There is a condition to this new start, which is submission to God's ways. This implies an acknowledgement of being wrong in the past. It is what the Bible calls confession of sin. There is also a consequence of refusing God's way.

God's way of salvation is reasonable because it alone deals with the real issues. It is not an empty sentimental way but one that offers a real solution to the problem of human sin.

12.

AN UNPOPULAR WAY

'He was despised and rejected by men'
(Isaiah 53:3).

12.

An unpopular way

Everything we have seen so far about God's way of salvation has shown that it is contrary to what the human heart and mind would have expected. One result of this is that God's way is not popular. This unpopularity is true with those who are opposed to any religion, but also with those who give an outward allegiance, not only to religion in general, but to Christianity in particular. We can see this very clearly in John chapter 6 when Jesus spoke of himself as the Bread of Life. Those who up to this point had been ardent followers of Jesus found this teaching offensive and turned away from him.

An offensive teaching

The incident in John 6 took place just before the Passover (v. 4), that is, exactly one year before the crucifixion. It happened in Capernaum, therefore among people who for the past two years had been Christ's greatest supporters. In the crowd were three distinct groups of hearers. There were the Jews (v. 41). These were the religious establishment who were always opposed to Jesus. Then there were those called the 'disciples' (vv. 60-61). These have to be distinguished from the 'Twelve' (v. 67), who were the apostles.

The disciples were the majority of the crowd and it was these who were offended at what the Lord taught that day. They found it hard and unacceptable. This is strange because up to this point there seemed to be no limit to their support and admiration of Jesus. They had been among the 5000 who had been miraculously fed and they were willing to use force to make Jesus king (v. 15). So these people were no casual hangers on. They followed Jesus everywhere (v. 24). As long as things were happening, as long as there was excitement and activity, these folk were there (vv. 2, 14). They hankered for the spectacular and dramatic (v. 30), but Jesus did not encourage this.

Jesus then began to teach them basic, solid, essential doctrine. He began to make demands upon them to think. The miracles should have made them think but their reaction to these had been carnal (v. 26). During the teaching sessions, the Jews became more vocal and the disciples just listened. They listen but they do not like what they are hearing. They said, 'This is a hard teaching. Who can accept it?' (v. 60). It is clear from verse 52 that when Jesus said he was the Bread of Life that they needed to eat, these people took Jesus literally. They thought he was advocating some sort of cannibalism. They completely misunderstood but instead of making it easier for them, Jesus immediately seems to go out of his way to make things more difficult. He does not tone down his earlier statement but strengthens it by saying that they must also drink his blood. What was difficult becomes impossible for these Jewish disciples.

Why did Jesus do this? Even though he is debating with the Jews, his aim was to speak to the crowd of previously enthusiastic disciples. He wanted to show them where they truly are spiritually. A man's true spiritual condition is not revealed by his reaction to what Jesus did — who can quarrel with the sick being healed? Our spiritual condition is to be measured by how we react to the teaching and doctrine of Jesus.

Today there are many who call themselves Christians and delight in healings and miracles; but when it comes to the doctrine of Jesus, particularly his teaching on the way of salvation, they are offended. The offence in John 6 was caused by what Jesus said about the sovereignty of God in salvation and about he himself being the only way of salvation. This was not popular and therefore was unacceptable.

Only God can save

It is amazing how many people are offended when told that they cannot save themselves, cannot deal with their own sin and cannot make themselves acceptable to God. This is exactly what Jesus taught: 'No one can come to me unless the Father who sent me draws him' (v. 44). To make sure we take this seriously he repeats it in verse 65.

Why can't the sinner come to God? Because he is dead in sin (Ephesians 2:1). This means he is spiritually helpless. So helpless, in fact, that Paul puts it like this in Romans 8:6-8: 'The mind of sinful man is death, but the mind controlled by the Spirit is life and peace; the sinful mind is hostile to God. It does not submit to God's law, nor can it do so. Those controlled by the sinful nature cannot please God.' This is very real. The gospel always kicks away the crutches that the sinner likes to lean on — good works, religious adherence and morality. It leaves him with nowhere to go except to the only person God has provided to deal with our sin. God overcomes our helplessness by drawing us to himself.

Drawing is the work of the Holy Spirit through the preaching of the gospel. The Spirit and the truth together create a conviction of sin in the heart. A deep longing, as distinct to a casual interest, for salvation develops. This is all part of God's way of salvation and without it we have no hope. It is unpopular because we like to think that we are in control of our own lives. It seems logical to us to assume that we must in some way earn our salvation. We must at least be able to contribute to it. But the gospel says this is all wrong. We bring nothing to our salvation except the sin we need to be saved from.

A great preacher of the nineteenth century once said that a man is never so near to grace as when he realizes he can do nothing. This teaching is hard to some and deeply offensive to others, but it is God's way.

God only saves through Jesus

Eating the flesh and drinking the blood of Jesus was symbolic language for a direct participation in and benefit from the death of Jesus on the cross, where his body was broken and his blood shed. It is another way of saying that we must believe in Jesus alone for salvation. Wherever you go in the New Testament you always come back to this basic fact.

If we take this out of the gospel, what are we left with? We would have a message as empty as it is useless. It would probably be popular with a great many people because it would be pliable and easily suited to meet any viewpoint. The Jesus of the New Testament and his cross are not like that. The cross is an ugly, violent place, which demands death. There is nothing romantic or sentimental about a crucifixion. The cross is uncompromising and accepts no half measures. It denounces sin and pays out sin's wage to the full. But this is where the sinner's only hope lies.

Borne by Jesus our sin is dealt with once and for all. The demand was total, the price paid was absolute — Jesus died for sinners. Anything less would have been unacceptable to God and anything more was impossible. It may not be popular but it is God's way and it is our only hope. To try and amend the gospel is to accuse God of doing what was unnecessary. To try and improve on it is like lighting one small candle to supplement the sun.

The gospel was complete the moment Jesus died and rose from the dead. What Jesus did on Calvary is sufficient to deal with our sin once and for all.

13.

A HAPPY WAY

'Therefore, there is now no condemnation for those who are in Christ Jesus' (Romans 8:1).

13.

A happy way

Happiness is a very flimsy thing. For most folk it depends upon circumstances. If a man wins the lottery happiness is guaranteed, but if he loses his job or his health declines then happiness will not be possible. By this standard, happiness is a fleeting allusion, always dancing in and out of our lives and never constant or permanent. In contrast, the Bible tells us that God's way is a truly happy one. This happiness is not an end in itself; rather it is a by-product of something more basic and more important.

The first psalm tells us clearly what makes a man happy. The psalmist says that happiness depends upon our relationship to God.

The wrong way

The happy man is someone who does not do certain things. The world does not like negatives especially in the area of moral behaviour and thinking. It finds them restrictive. The negative is frowned upon as being a miserable way to live. But the Bible is always using negatives to make its point. For instance, in the Ten Commandments God could easily have said that we must be honest. Instead he said, 'You shall not steal.' He could have said that we must respect our marriage vows, but instead he said, 'You shall not commit adultery.' By using the negative the truth is emphasized and no one can misunderstand.

The happy man 'does not walk in the counsel of the wicked or stand in the way of sinners or sit in the seat of mockers' (Psalm 1:1).

Not walking in the counsel of the wicked means that he does not take his standards and behavioural pattern from the current whim of the world. Trendy TV producers and godless newspaper editors are not allowed to mould his thinking. This being true he does not stand or sit, make himself at home, with the godless attitudes of the broad way.

The person consumed with admiration for the broad way will never be happy because the happiness it offers is one massive delusion. The world will never know real happiness simply because it is preoccupied with it. Its so-called happiness is therefore always shallow and artificial, always dependent upon circumstances. It is not difficult to prove this. Just consider the sort of people the TV and newspapers always hold up to us as ones to be admired and if possible to be imitated. The so-called stars are so happy that they cannot exist without drugs, excessive drinking and three or four marriages. That's the type of happiness we are better off without.

The right way

What is it that makes a man happy? It is to experience God's way of salvation and live to please God. Psalm 1 puts it like this: 'his delight is in the law of the Lord, and on his law he meditates day and night' (v. 2).

To many people nothing could be more dreary and boring than this. To a man on the broad way such a conclusion is inevitable. Such concepts are foreign to him but at one time they were foreign to us all. No one naturally lives like this. This pattern of behaviour is found only on the other side of the narrow gate.

Here is a man who takes his standards, thinking and attitudes from the revealed will of God. This means he has a standard that does not change. This is exactly the opposite of the world whose standards are chang-ing all the time. Also he has a standard outside of himself and therefore not dictated by his own weaknesses and prejudices. This gives an authority and purpose to his life.

Such a man takes God seriously. He does not play at religion. Christianity is not a hobby to him but the centre of his life. It is possible to be in church every Sunday and still take your standards from the world. It is also possible to call yourself a Christian and not delight in the law of the Lord. These things are possible if a man has no real relationship with God. His religion is as empty as another man's life of drink and sex.

Happiness is...

1. Having your greatest problem dealt with.

Life is full of problems and no one avoids them. But the greatest problem by far is the one of our own personal sin and guilt. Unless this is dealt with it will take us to hell for eternity.

All people are by nature great optimists when it comes to God. They think that in the end everything will be all right. They know they are not as good as they should be, but there are plenty of people far worse than them so, they think, God is bound to accept them. It is only when a man begins to listen to what God says in the

Bible that this false optimism disappears. He sees there how seriously God takes sin and this shakes him. What use is it being as good as the next man if that man is going to hell?

A veneer of happiness can be maintained by ignoring what God says. After all, judgement and hell are considered to be old-fashioned and outdated beliefs. But the trouble is that death is not old-fashioned and it is coming to us all. Death, no matter what men may say, makes judgement and hell very real. The happy man is the one who knows that death holds no terror for him because his sin has been dealt with once and for all by the Lord Jesus Christ.

2. Having a peace that no one can take away.

The peace God gives us is not dependent upon circumstances but upon the eternal worth of what Christ has done for us. It is the peace that does not disappear when life gets rough. Jesus promised us that what he gives us, thieves will never be able to steal and moth and rust never be able to destroy.

God's way is the way of life more abundant. This does not mean that it is littered with gadgets and material possessions but filled with the reality of God. No wonder the man who knows this is happy.

3. Having a guaranteed future.

For most people the future means from now until the grave. For the Christian it means from now and for all eternity.

Guarantees are notoriously unreliable things. We are urged to read the small print to be sure of the terms. Very few things are guaranteed for life and when things do go wrong it is not always easy to claim on your guarantee. Perhaps it has run out or the particular part you need is not covered. We have all known this. But God's guarantee has no small print, there is no time limit and everything is covered. It depends upon the unfailing love of God in Christ. Those on God's way are saved for eternity. Heaven is guaranteed them and there are no catches. It is true happiness to know this.

Some people want to dismiss Christianity as 'pie in the sky when you die', and choose instead to live out the false illusion and flimsy happiness of being in this world without God. But being without God is also to be without hope and that is the most terrible of all situations.

The Christian's happiness is not obtained only when he reaches heaven but the moment he steps through the narrow gate onto God's way.

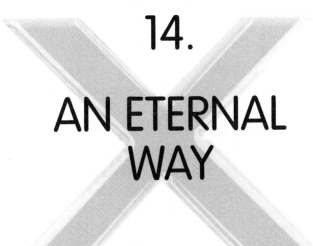

14.

AN ETERNAL WAY

*'I tell you the truth, he who believes has
everlasting life'* (John 6:47).

14.

An eternal way

Jesus is described in Hebrews 5:9 as 'the source of eternal salvation'. He is not the source merely of salvation but of a salvation that is eternal. This is what Jesus himself claimed in John 10:28: 'I give them eternal life.' Paul delights in the same truth at the end of Romans 8 where he says that nothing will be able to separate us from the love of God that is in Christ Jesus our Lord.

The important thing about a way is its destination, and God's way of salvation leads to life. Because that life is eternal life the way is actually endless. It keeps us forever in fellowship with God. There is no end to the saving relationship between God and the redeemed sinner. This has to be a great comfort to every believer. To have salvation is a great thing, but to know you can never lose it is even greater. This sounds too good to be true but true it is, and Hebrews 6 sets before us the ground or basis of this most comforting thought. It rests upon three things.

1. *What God calls us* ('The heirs of what was promised',
   v. 17).

Much is made in Hebrews 6 of the promise of God. We
are told in verse 13 that God made a promise to
Abraham. In the next verse we see what that promise
was as the writer quotes from Genesis 22:17: 'I will
surely bless you and give you many descendants.' Paul
refers to this promise when he says in Romans 4:11
that Abraham is the father of all who believe. In
Galatians 3:7-8 he also quotes from Genesis 22 but
this time it is from verse 18: 'Understand, then, that
those who believe are children of Abraham. The Scripture foresaw that God would justify the Gentiles by faith,
and announced the gospel in advance to Abraham: "All
nations will be blessed through you."'

So the promise to Abraham contained an advance
notice of the gospel. This is developed in Galatians 3:14:
'He redeemed us in order that the blessing given to
Abraham might come to the Gentiles through Christ
Jesus, so that by faith we might receive the promise of
the Spirit.' The Christian is an heir of the promise of the
gospel, the promise of salvation.

An heir is someone who has been chosen. Very
often the heir is a member of the family, but not
always. Either way, when a man makes a will he

names his heir. By definition an heir is someone with something coming to him. He may not have it yet but it is promised to him. He may be unaware that he is an heir but he will receive what is promised at the right time.

Even before they were saved, all Christians were heirs of salvation. They did not know it but they had been chosen. God had promised them something only he could give. God the author and source of salvation had chosen them in Christ before the foundation of the world. This is the message of the gospel. The first gospel announcement in the New Testament said, 'He will save his people from their sins' (Matthew 1:21). Jesus will save because God had promised it, and they are his people because they are heirs, chosen by God.

Salvation, says Hebrews 6:17, springs out of the purpose of God. 'Purpose' there means, as it does everywhere in the New Testament, the eternal decree or choice of God (Acts 2:23; Ephesians 1:9-11). The difference between the purpose of God and the promise of God is that the purpose is a secret hidden in the heart of God and the promise is the open declaration of that purpose. God promises what he has already decided to do.

2. What the Holy Spirit led us to do ('We who have fled to take hold of the hope offered to us', v. 18).

The hope is Christ himself and Christ is set forth in the gospel. So to be saved a sinner must hear the gospel; but hearing is not enough.

A man hears the gospel and pays no attention to it. He regards it as irrelevant and dismisses it as nonsense.

Another man hears the gospel and shows an interest in it but he is not serious. He believes what is told him, but because he is, by his own reckoning, a good man, he does not feel the need for a saviour.

Another man hears and at one time he may have been exactly like the other two, but now the Holy Spirit begins to speak to his heart and conscience. He sees his sin and feels a desperate need for salvation. He is in the world without God and without hope. He sees himself having to stand before the judgement seat of God. He realizes that all his sin has to be answered for and he has no answer and no excuse. His own heart condemns him and he knows he deserves hell.

All this is created in his heart and mind by the Holy Spirit. But because God is doing this he is not left in despair. He is led to see that his only hope is in Jesus who died for sinners. So he is now aware of the love and mercy that is in Christ and, with judgement hovering over him, he can do only one thing — he flees to Christ to take hold of this hope, this promise, this salvation.

He does not merely want to hear about it, or to admire it, or to sing of it, he wants to possess it. There is an urgency and a desperation so he flees to Christ. Several years ago I had a heart attack and an ambulance was sent to take me to hospital. When we set off for the hospital with the blue lamp flashing, the driver did not go at a leisurely 20mph, nor did he stop for traffic lights. This was urgent and nothing was allowed to delay him getting me to hospital. It was a matter of life and death. When a sinner is convicted of his sin and the reality of God's judgement, he flees to Christ. There is nothing more urgent. He would be a fool to delay. Because the Holy Spirit is working within him, salvation has become to him the only thing that matters.

3. What God does for us now ('greatly encouraged',
        v. 18).

The only one who will flee to Christ is the one conscious of his sin and the only encouragement he wants is to be certain that his sin is forgiven now and for ever. This certainty is contained in the gospel: 'Because God wanted to make the unchanging nature of his purpose very clear to the heirs of what was promised, he confirmed it with an oath. God did this so that, by two unchangeable things in which it is impossible for God to lie, we who have fled to take hold of the hope offered to us may be greatly encouraged' (Hebrews 6:17-18).

Our encouragement is in the two unchangeable things that God has done. God knows how so full of doubts and fears we are, so he wanted to make 'the unchanging nature of his purpose very clear' to us. The unchanging nature of his purpose of salvation means that once we are saved we are always saved. That is what he promised and, so that we would be certain of this, he confirmed it with an oath. God did not have to do this: you only require an oath from someone if you are not sure if they are telling the truth. But this is God who cannot lie. Who can doubt the promise of God? The simple answer is that we can and often do. So God, aware of our dullness and unbelief, makes an oath to confirm that this is the truth.

The 'two unchangeable things in which it is impossible for God to lie' are his promise and his oath. Our encouragement is that we are saved for eternity.

The encouragement is further strengthened in verse 19 when we are told that we have the hope of the gospel as an anchor for our soul. An anchor is used to secure a ship in times of storm. It prevents the ship from drifting from its moorings. The anchor is invisible, hidden beneath the waves where it grips the seabed. The storm will roar and batter the ship. Enormous forces are at work to move the vessel but though it may move a little, the anchor holds it firm and secure.

The storms of life batter the Christian. Pressures, stresses, anxieties all work to destroy his faith. We are tempted to move away from God but Christ our hope, our anchor, holds us firm. The anchor is fixed in heaven itself, so nothing that happens in this world can move it. Our security is outside of ourselves. It does not depend upon us but upon the triumphant, ascended and glorified Christ.

15.

A WELCOMING WAY

'Come to me, all you who are weary and burdened, and I will give you rest'
(Matthew 11:28).

15.

A welcoming way

You will have gathered that I survived that heart attack. The ambulance got me to hospital in time and the doctors did the rest. The question now is, will you survive the disease of sin that fills your heart?

We have seen many things about God's way of salvation but, to end with, it is important that we see it is a welcoming way. It is not hidden, not obscure, but open and welcoming. For two thousand years God has preserved his gospel from all the attacks of men and you have been confronted with it in this book. You may have heard it before but you may still not be on God's way. You must be in no doubt that God wants you to be on his way.

In the Old Testament God pleads with sinners: 'Therefore, O house of Israel, I will judge you, each one according to his ways, declares the Sovereign LORD. Repent! Turn away from all your offences; then sin will not be your downfall. Rid yourselves of all the offences you have committed, and get a new heart and a new spirit. Why will you die, O house of Israel? For I take no pleasure in the death of anyone, declares the Sovereign LORD. Repent and live!' (Ezekiel 18:30-32).

In the New Testament Jesus does the same thing: 'O Jerusalem, Jerusalem, you who kill the prophets and stone those sent to you, how often I have longed to gather your children together, as a hen gathers her chicks under her wings, but you were not willing!' (Luke 13:34).

Both passages show the concern God has for men and women to be saved, and he is concerned about your salvation. He wants you to come in repentance and faith to Jesus. In the parable of the prodigal son, Jesus shows us something of God's welcome for sinners in the attitude of the prodigal's father when his son returned: 'But while he was still a long way off, his father saw him and was filled with compassion for him; he ran to his son, threw his arms around him and kissed him' (Luke 15:20).

There is a chain of hotels in the USA called Welcome Inns. They supply a good service to their customers and because of this are very popular. But there must be times when travellers have to be turned away because they are full up. No establishment has limitless accommodation and the better the service the more likely they are to be full.

No one is turned away by God. There is always plenty of room, and what he supplies is beyond comparison. There is room for every sinner who comes looking for grace and salvation.

The welcome with God is warm and enthusiastic, but that in no way tones down the condition of entrance. We must go through the narrow gate to get onto God's way. Jesus is the only way and the gospel tells us all we need to know about him.

Find out more about God's Word in this easy-to-read little book!

AN ABC OF THE CHRISTIAN FAITH BY **PETER JEFFERY**

bitesize
theology

In this easy-to-read book, Peter Jeffery shows us just how tantalizingly enjoyable Bible teaching can be. With short but solid chapters on key subjects, he outlines the ABCs of the Christian faith.

Each of the chapters is bite-sized. There is just enough to manage at one time, and you will find there is much to nourish the mind as well as warm the heart and inspire the will. It includes a guide for reading the New Testament and Psalms in a year.

Bitesize theology, Peter Jeffery, ISBN 0 85234 447 3, 112pp, also published by Evangelical Press.

A wide range of excellent books on spiritual subjects is available from Evangelical Press. Please write to us for your free catalogue or contact us by e-mail.

Evangelical Press
Faverdale North Industrial Estate, Darlington, Co. Durham, DL3 0PH, England

Evangelical Press USA
P. O. Box 84, Auburn, MA 01501, USA

e-mail: sales@evangelical-press.org

web: www.evangelical-press.org